FIRST BOOK OF
NUMBERS

PRACTICE IN WRITING NUMBERS AND COUNTING 1 TO 20

illustrated by Lois Ehlert

3 skating bears

©1992, 1982 Western Publishing Company, Inc.
All Rights Reserved.

All trademarks are the property of Western Publishing Company, Inc.

A GOLDEN BOOK®
Western Publishing Company, Inc.
Racine, Wisconsin 53404
No part of this book may be reproduced or copied in any form
without written permission from the publisher. Produced in U.S.A.

Follow the arrows to write numbers 1 to 10.

Say their names.

Copy the numbers.

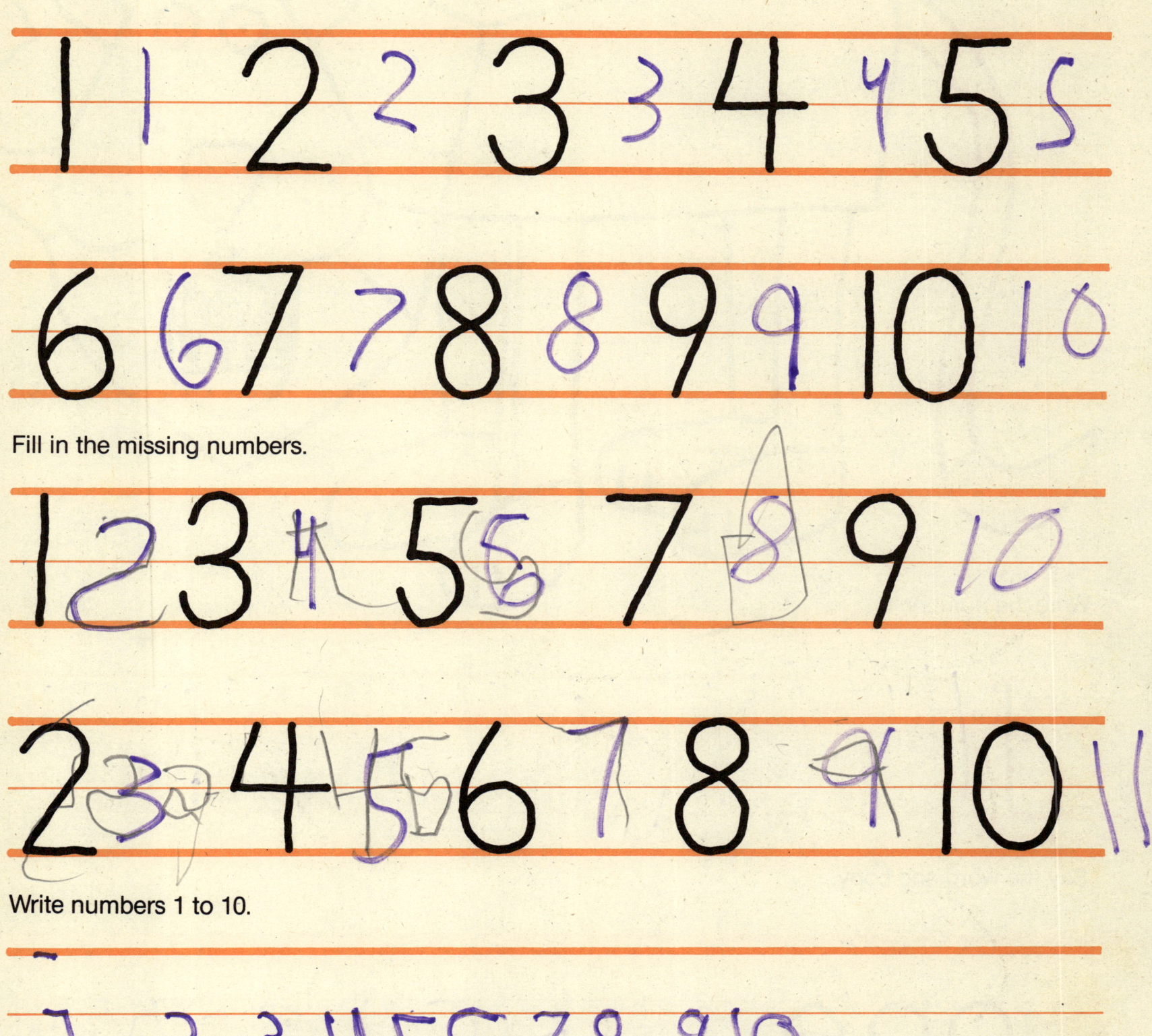

Fill in the missing numbers.

Write numbers 1 to 10.

Here is **1** **lion.**

Write the number 1.

Say the word and copy.

one one one on one

2 tigers

Write the number 2.

2 2 2 2 2 2 2

Say the word and copy.

two two two

3 skating bears

Write the number 3.

3

Say the word and copy.

three

4 performing elephants

Write the number 4.

4

Say the word and copy.

four

5 dancing dogs

Write the number 5.

5

Say the word and copy.

five

6 acrobats

Write the number 6.

6

Say the word and copy.

six

7 silly clowns

Write the number 7.

7

Say the word and copy.

seven

8 trained horses

Write the number 8.

8

Say the word and copy.

eight

9 balls for the juggler to juggle

Write the number 9.

9

Say the word and copy.

nine

10 circus hats

Write the number 10.

10

Say the word and copy.

ten

How many bones? 6

How many dogs? 6

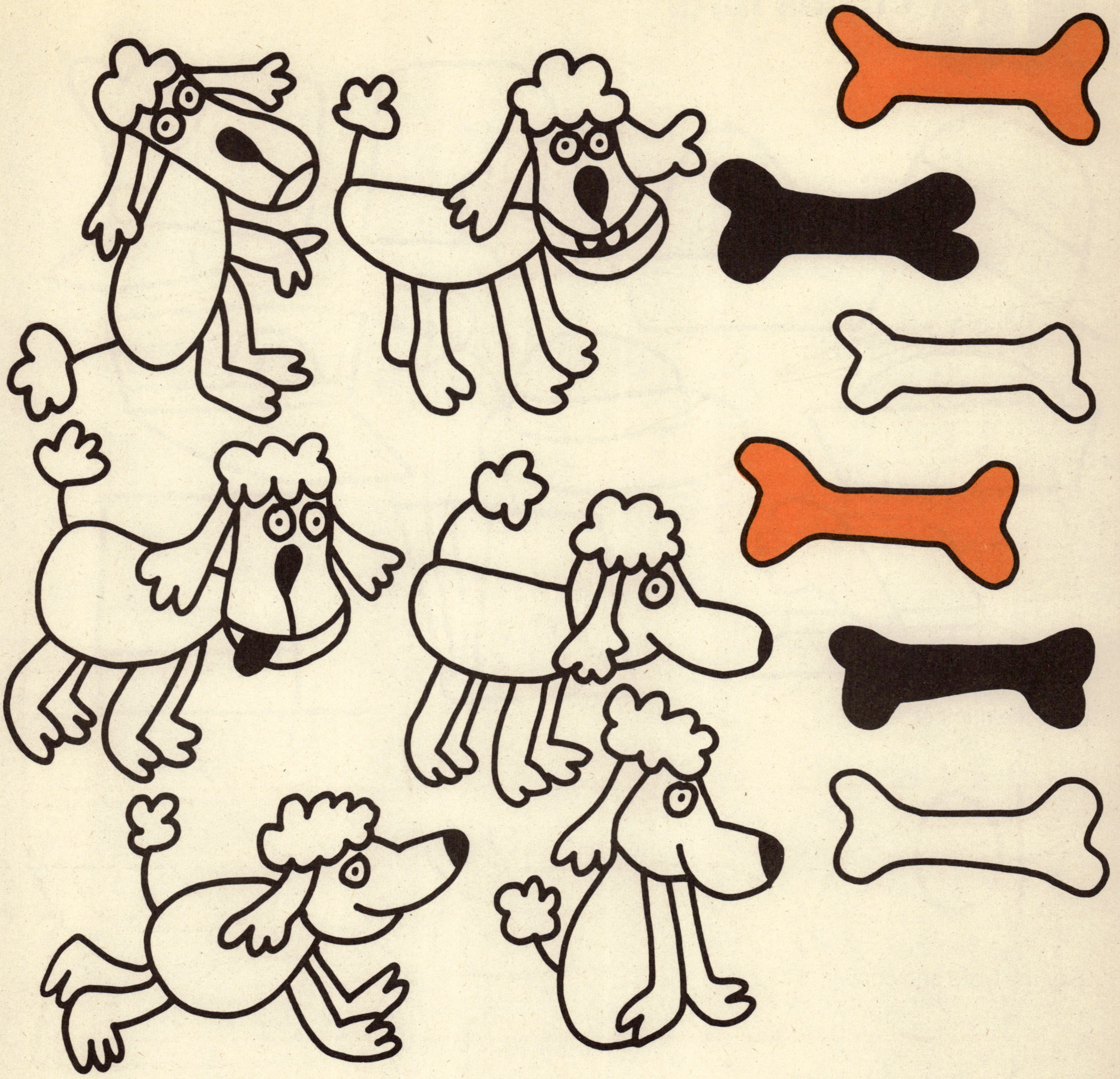

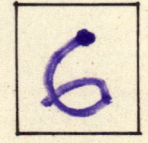

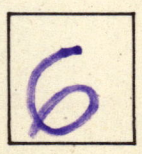

How many tigers? 3   How many stands? 2

What is missing?   Can you draw another stand?

stand

Draw a line to match the sets that have the same numbers of objects.

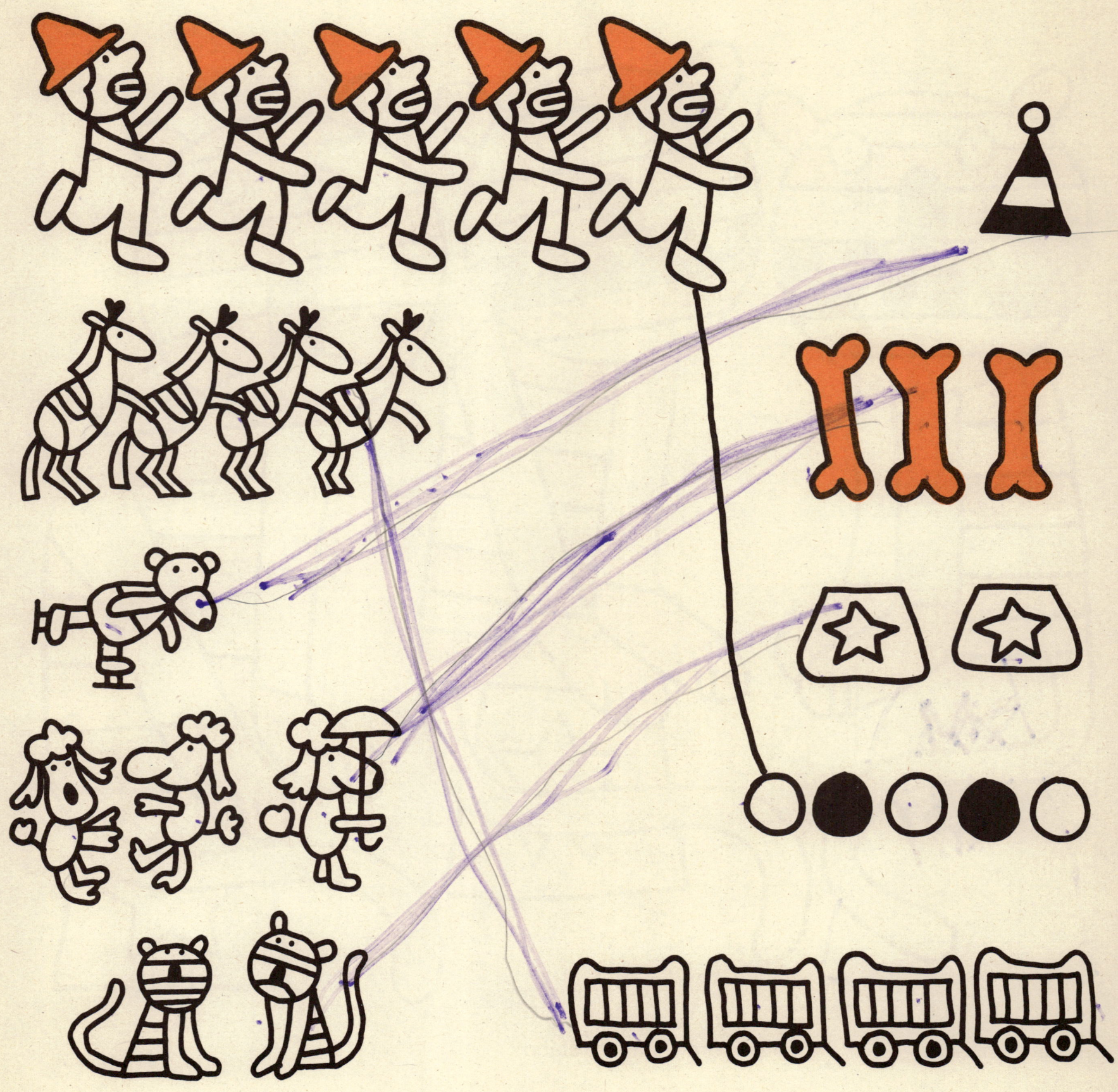

How many?   Draw a circle around the right number.

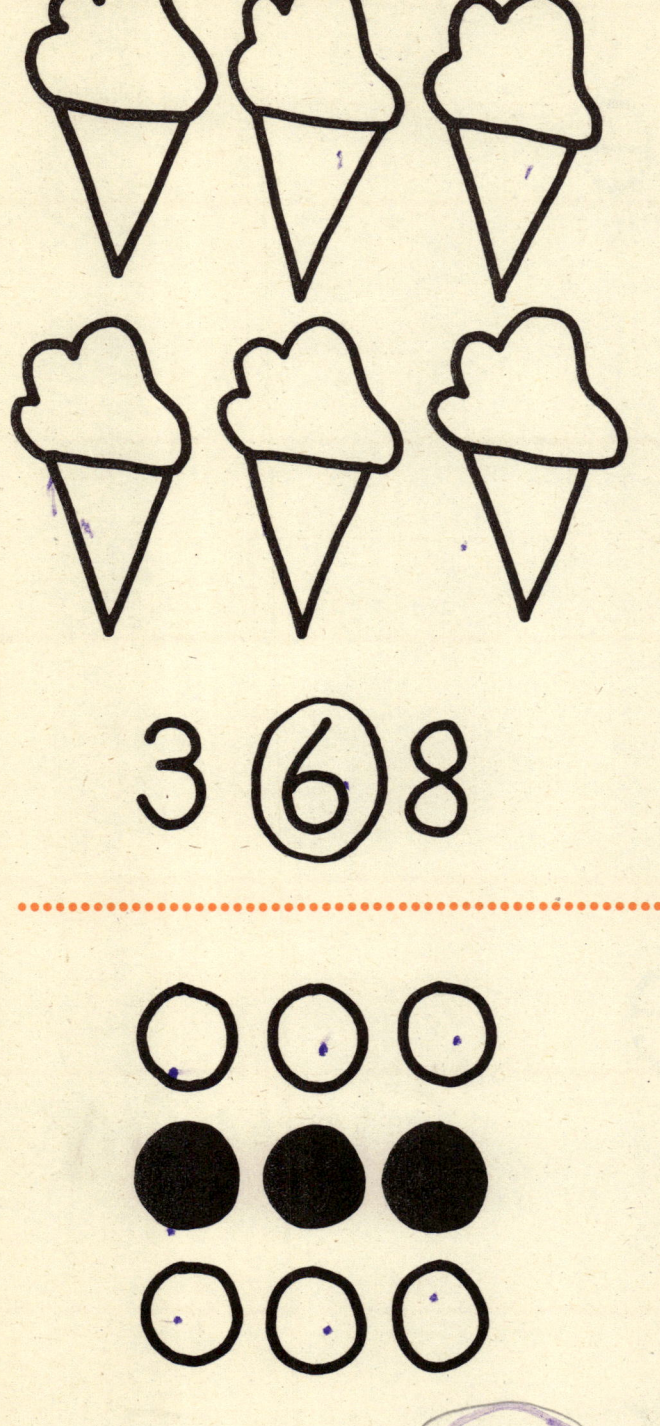

Count the objects and draw a line to the number word.   Copy the number words.

Draw and Color.

Draw 3 more balls like this:

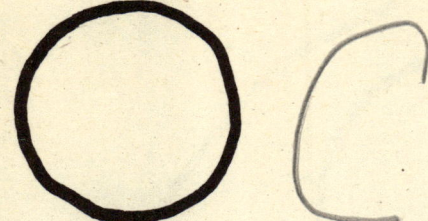

How many balls?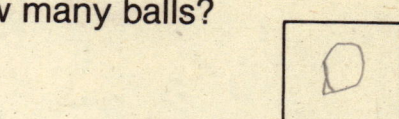

Draw 5 more circus pennants like this:

How many pennants?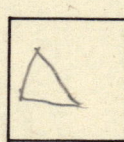

Draw 6 more ringmaster hats like this:

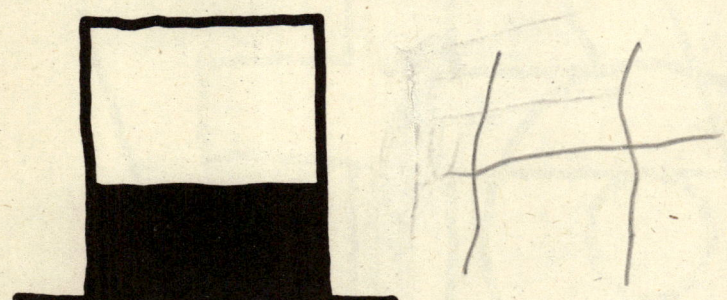

How many hats?

Draw 4 more drums like this:

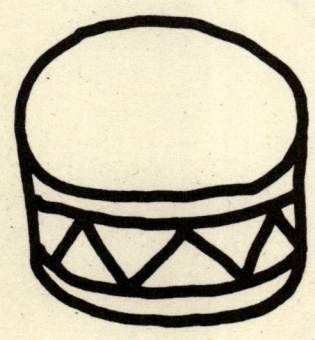 

How many drums?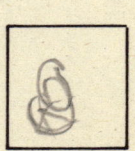

Find and color the numbers 1 to 9 in the crystal ball.

How many flowers on the gypsy's scarf? □   How many beads on her necklace? □

How many circus pennants? ☐ How many cotton candies? ☐

How many sodas? ☐

Follow the dots 1 to 10.   1 2 3 4 5 6 7 8 9 10

How many balloons?

Count on the clown.

How many eyes? ☐   How many noses? ☐   How many arms? ☐

How many hands? ☐

How many fingers? ☐   How many legs? ☐

How many feet? ☐

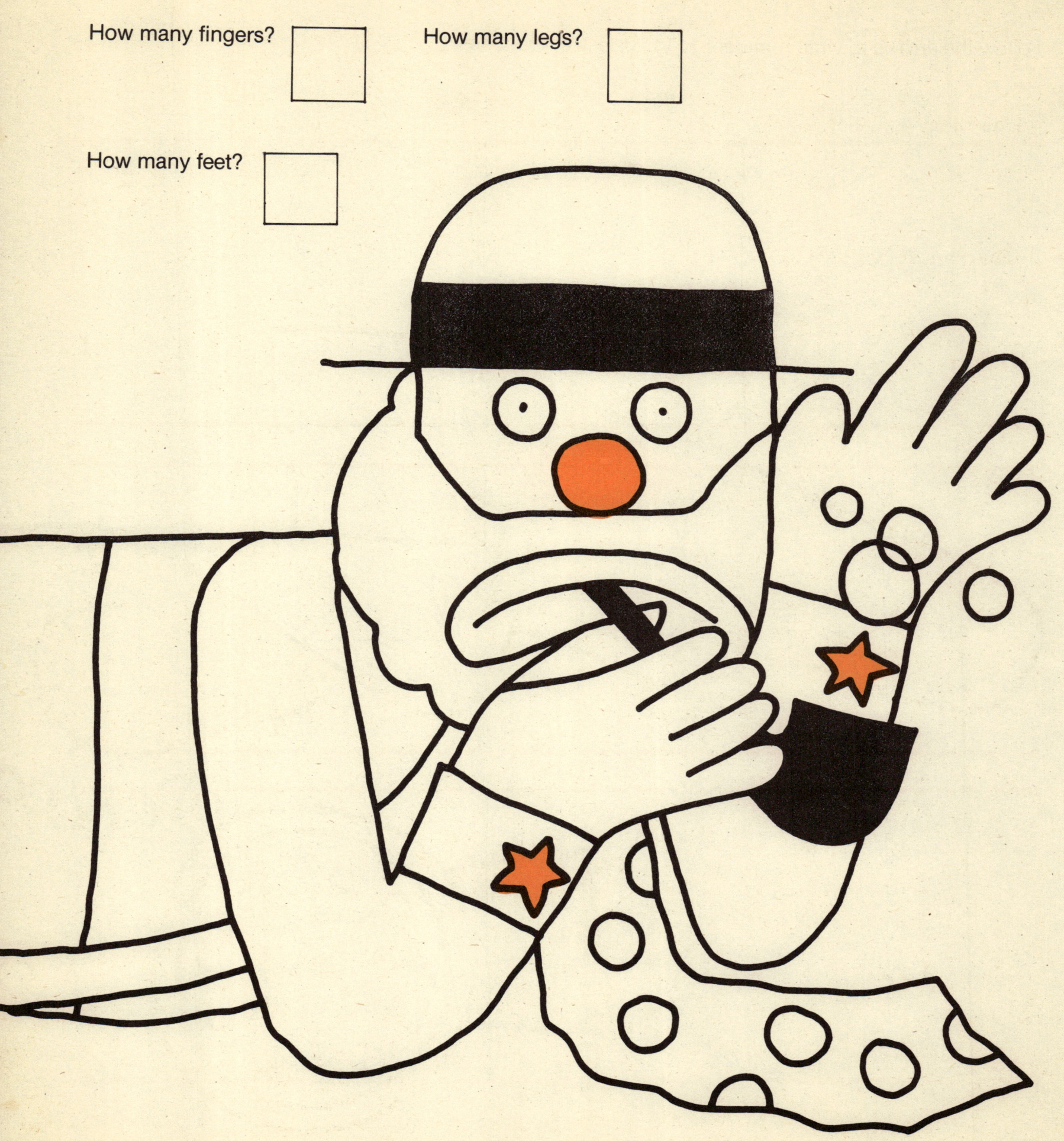

Follow the arrows to write numbers 11 to 20. Say their names.

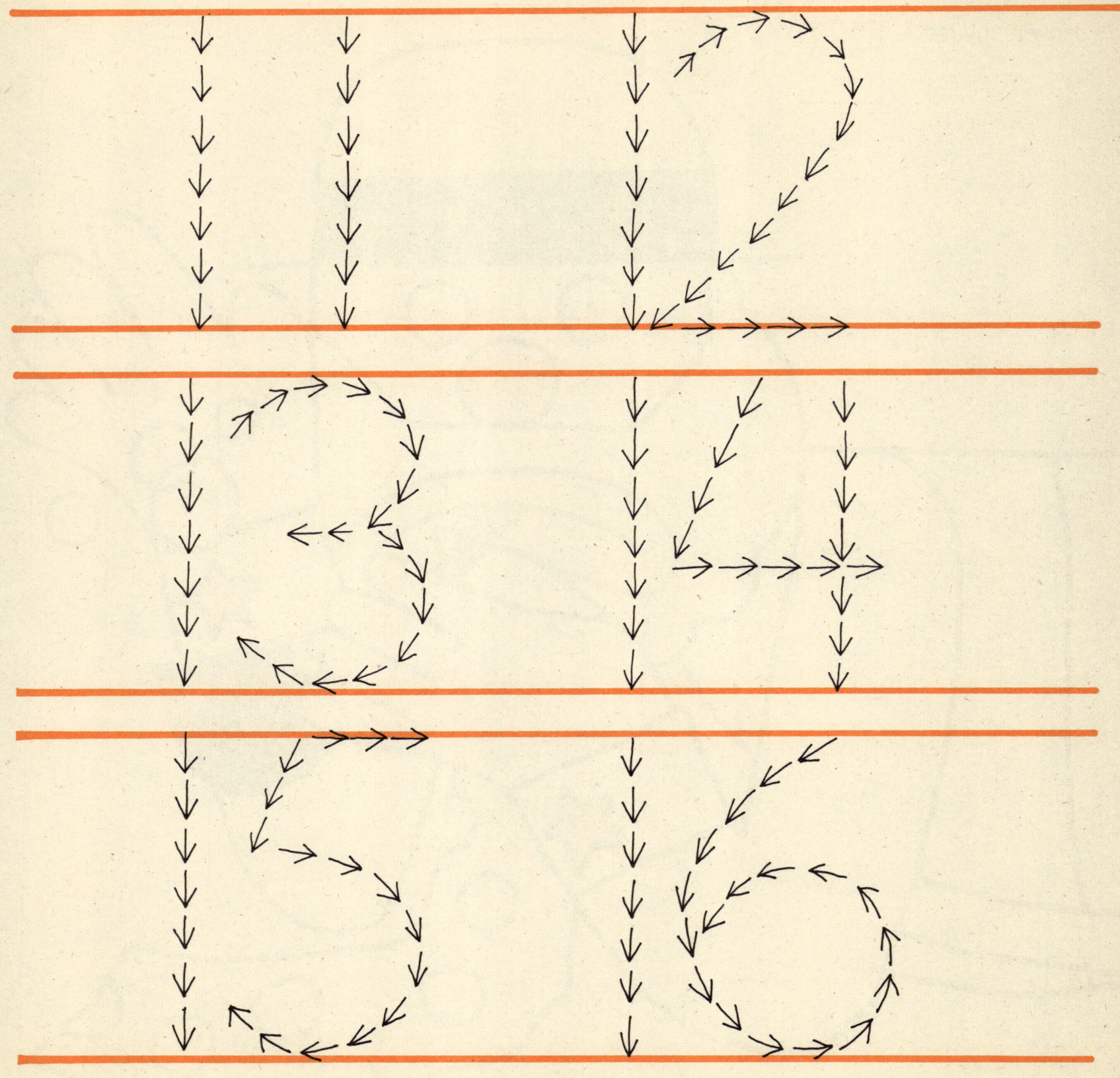

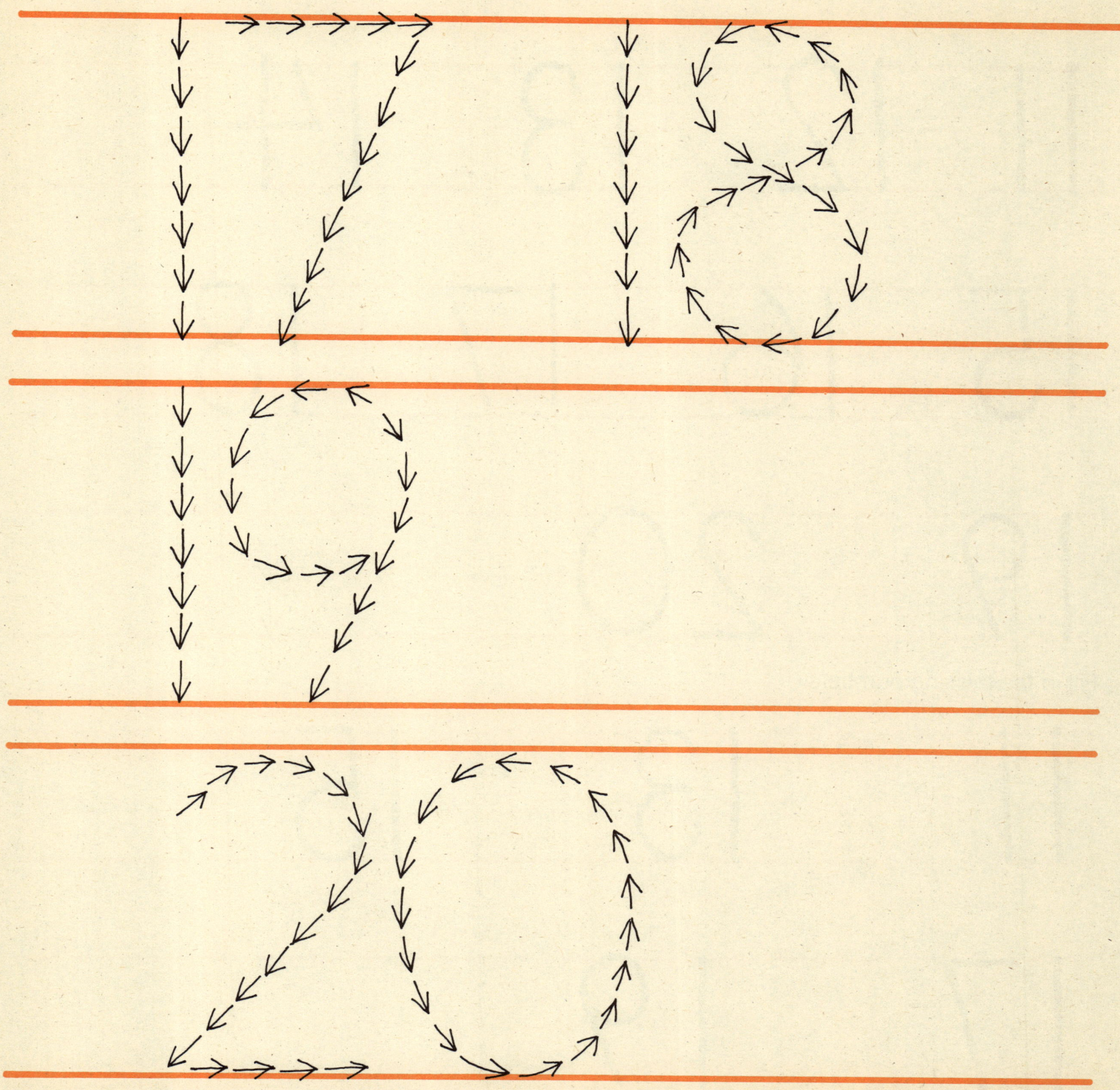

Copy numbers 11 to 20.

11 12 13 14

15 16 17 18

19 20

Fill in the missing numbers.

11 ___ 13 ___ 15

___ 17 ___ 19 ___

Write the numbers.

11

12

13

14

15

Write the numbers.

16

17

18

19

20

The clown magician is going to show you about numbers 11 to 20.

Count what he pulls from his hat.

Copy the numbers.

11

12

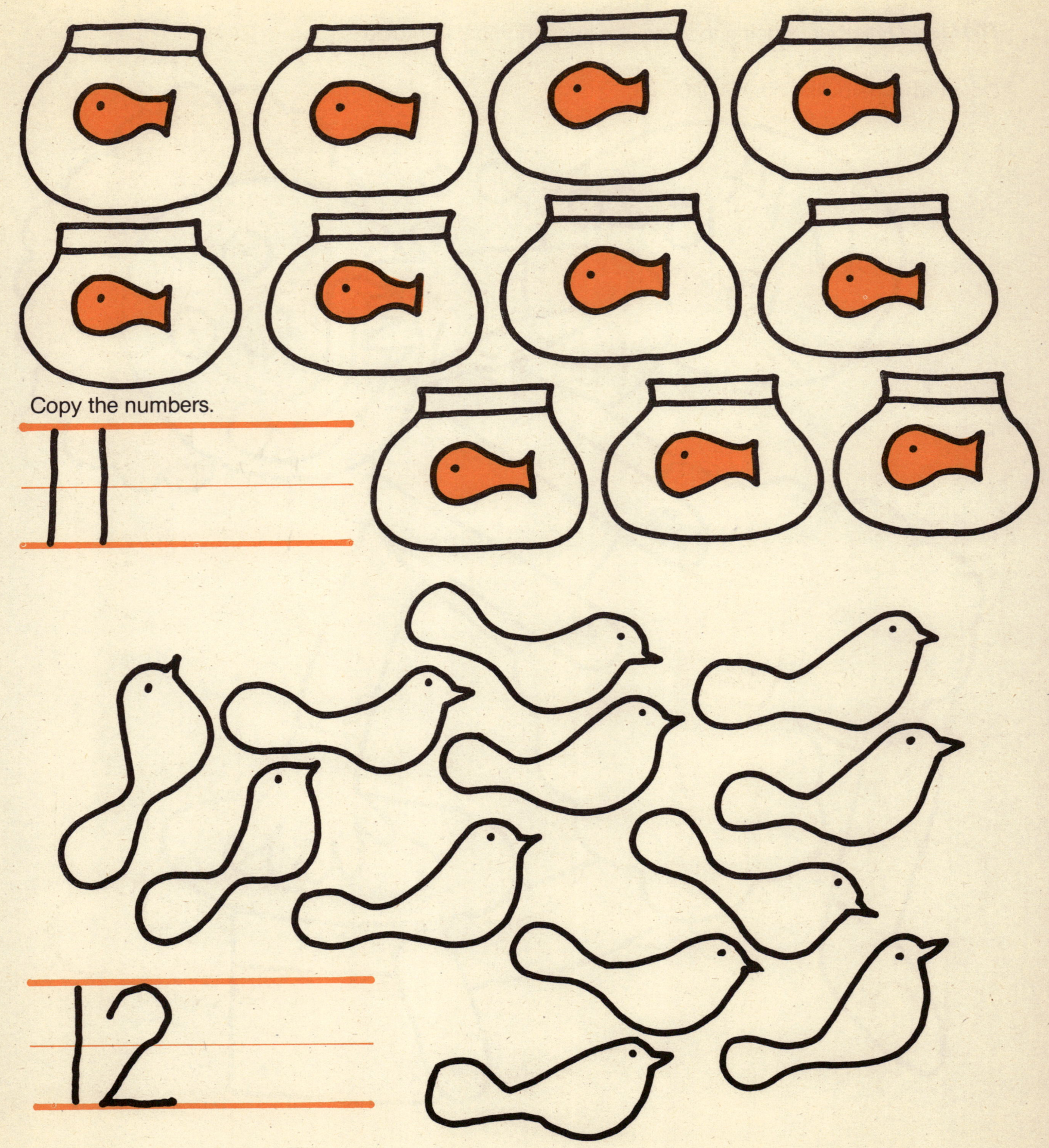

14 14

15 15

18 | 8
19 | 9

20 20

Count the stars on the circus poster. How many stars?

BINGLING CIRCUS

Follow the dots 1 to 20.

BINGLING CIRCUS

Draw a line from the number to the set with that many objects.

15

18

14

Follow the dots 1 to 12 to find out who is with the lion.

Follow the dots 1 to 15.

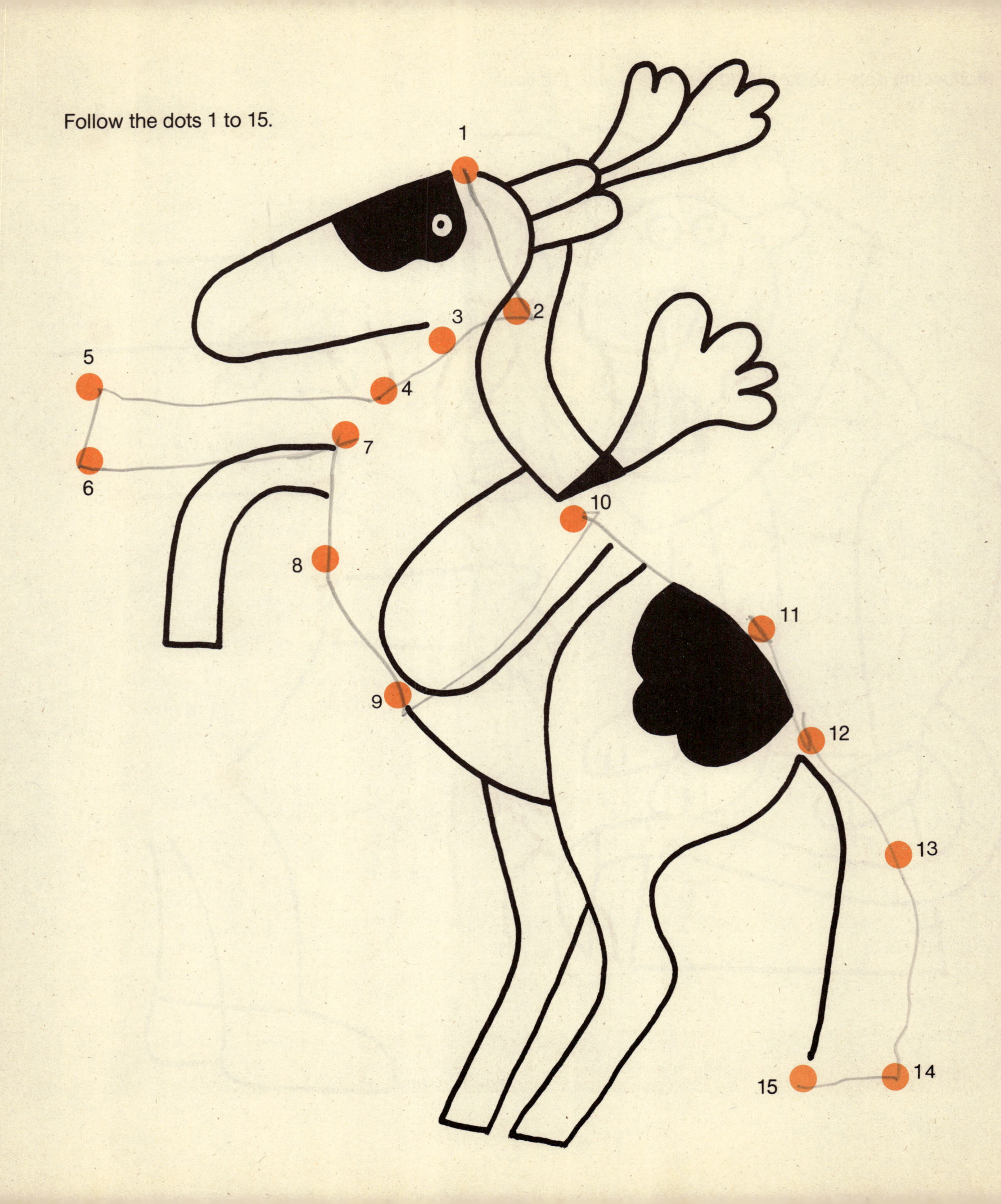

Find, count and color the balloons.

How many clowns in the circus band? ☐

How many horns? [5]   How many drums? [5]

How many dots on the wagon? [5]

Follow the path to the circus. Fill in the missing numbers.

1 2 3 4 5 6 7 8 9 10 11 12 13 14 15 16 17 18 19 20

This is a circus birthday cake. How many candles would you put on if it were your birthday?

Clocks have numbers too. What time does the circus start?

Add the hands.

Other numbers to know.

Fill in the blanks.

I am _____ years old.

My street number is _____.

My phone number is _____.

There are _____ people in my family

I am _____ inches tall.

I weigh _____ pounds.

My shoe size is _____.

I get up at _____ o'clock.

My birthday is _____.